HEALTH & FITNESS

HOW DOES MY
DIET
AFFECT ME?

Patsy Westcott

HODDER
Wayland

an imprint of Hodder Children's Books

HOW DOES ADOLESCENCE AFFECT ME?
HOW DO DRINK AND DRUGS AFFECT ME?
HOW DOES EXERCISE AFFECT ME?
HOW DOES MY DIET AFFECT ME?

Produced for Hodder Wayland Publishers Limited by
Roger Coote Publishing
Gissing's Farm
Fressingfield
Suffolk IP21 5SH
England

Designer: Victoria Webb
Editor: Steve Setford

First published in Great Britain in 1999 by Wayland (Publishers) Ltd
Reprinted in 2001 by Hodder Wayland,
an imprint of Hodder Children's Books

British Library Cataloguing in Publication Data
Westcott, Patsy
  How does my diet affect me?. – (Health and fitness)
  1.Diet – Juvenile literature 2.Nutrition – Juvenile literature
  I.Title
  613.2

ISBN 0 7502 2569 6

Printed and bound in Italy
by G. Canale & C.S.p.A., Turin

Acknowledgement
The author would like to thank dietitian Lyndel Costain of the British
Dietetic Association for her advice. Any opinions are the author's own.

Picture acknowledgements:
Digital Vision cover band (middle), 13 bottom, 15 top, 16-17, 19, 23 top, 27, 28 top; The Healthy Alliance/CCH
Communications 8; Image Bank 39 (Juan Silva); Science Photo Library 14 (Adrienne Hart-Davis), 17 top left
(Gaillard, Jerrican), 18 (Sheila Terry), 20 (Tony Craddock), 21 (Quest), 25 (BSIP Laurent H Americain), 28 bottom
(Damien Lovegrove), 32 (Clinical Radiology Dept, Salisbury District Hospital), 33 (Steve Horrell), 34 (John Bavosi),
43 (John Greim), 44 top (Dr P Marazzi), 44 bottom (Adrienne Hart-Davis), 45 (BSIP Edwige); Tony Stone Images
front cover (Paul Redman), 1 (Timothy Shonnard), 4 (Elie Bernager), 5 (Lori Adamski Peek), 6 (Leland Bobbe), 7
(Christopher Bissell), 10 (Ian Shaw), 12 (John Kelly), 13 top (Yann Layma), 17 top right (Christel Rosenfeld), 22-23
(Paul Chesley), 24 (Rosemary Weller), 26 (Warren Rosenberg), 30 (Dennis O'Clair), 31 (Lori Adamski Peek), 35
(Frank Siteman), 36 (Paul Webster), 37 (Ian O'Leary), 38 (Paul Redman), 40 (Steven Peters), 40-41 (Donna Day), 42
(Peter Cade); Wayland Picture Library cover band (bottom). The illustration on page 15 is by Peter Bull.

All Hodder Wayland books encourage children
to read and help them improve their literacy.

 The contents page, page numbers,
headings and index help locate
specific pieces of information.

 The glossary reinforces alphabetic
knowledge and extends vocabulary.

 The further information section sug-
gests other books dealing with the
same subject.

CONTENTS

WHY WE NEED FOOD

WHAT IS DIET?

Your body uses the food you eat to help you grow, to provide you with energy and to help you fight against infection and disease. The type and amount of food that we usually eat is known as our diet. Eating a healthy, varied diet will help to keep you strong and fit throughout your life. On the other hand, an unhealthy diet can lead to many problems and even shorten your life.

FOOD FOR LIFE

In order to live you need nutrients – nourishing substances that enable the cells of your body to work. Your body cannot make most of these nutrients, so you have to get them from the food you eat. The exact amount you need depends on your age, your size, how much you are growing, whether you are a boy or a girl, and how active you are.

FOOD FOR FUEL

Another important task of food is to provide your body with energy, which you need for activities such as walking, swimming, skating and dancing. But you also need energy for things that you rarely think about, such as breathing, digestion, keeping your heart beating and fuelling your brain. The energy in food is measured in units called calories. A slice and a half of bread contains about 100 calories. Any calories that your body does not use are stored as fat.

Left People of different ages need different amounts of food and nutrients.

Right The food you eat provides you with energy for all kinds of exercise and activity.

A BALANCED DIET

WHAT DETERMINES DIET?

People's diet varies greatly throughout the world. It depends largely on what foods grow locally, but customs, religious beliefs, regional tastes, and economics also determine what foods are eaten. Whatever foods are available, the secret of staying fit and healthy lies in making sure you have a balanced diet.

WHAT IS A BALANCED DIET?

A balanced diet provides you with just the right amount of nutrients and calories. Because just one food cannot give you all the nutrients you need, the best way to make sure you get enough nutrients is to eat a variety of different kinds of food. No foods are 'good' or 'bad' in themselves. The key thing is to get a good balance.

Your religion and your culture are among the many factors that affect the food you eat. Orthodox Jews, for example, do not eat pork, rabbit, shellfish and eels.

Always take a bottle of water with you when you exercise, particularly when it is hot, because you need to replace the water you lose when you sweat.

WATER – VITAL FOR LIFE

You can survive for quite a long while without food, but only for a short time without water. Water flushes waste products from your body and helps you dissolve and digest food. Lack of water can cause dry skin, dull hair and tiredness. You lose water when you sweat and when you urinate. You need more water during and after exercise, or if you have an illness that causes diarrhoea and vomiting. Water is found in food as well as drinks, especially in fruit and vegetables. A balanced diet with several glasses of water a day should give you enough.

TYPES OF NUTRIENTS

There are two main types of nutrients, known as macronutrients (macro means large) and micronutrients (micro means small). Proteins, carbohydrates and fats are macronutrients. You need quite large amounts of these nutrients for growth, development, body maintenance and energy. Micronutrients include forty-five or so vitamins, minerals and other substances that you require for many vital bodily processes. Although you only need these nutrients in very small quantities, without them the cells of your body cannot function properly.

FOOD GROUPS

Foods are classified into five different groups, based on the nutrients they provide. These are:

★ Bread, other cereals and potatoes
★ Fruit and vegetables
★ Milk and dairy foods
★ Meat, fish and alternatives
★ Fatty and sugary foods.

If you eat foods from each of the first four groups (not the fatty and sugary foods) every day you should have no problem staying healthy.

Fruit and vegetables
Foods in the fruit and vegetables group are a good source of carbohydrates, protein, minerals, vitamins and fibre. Aim to eat at least one food from this group at each meal and five servings every day. They make good snacks between meals too.

Bread, other cereals and potatoes
Foods in this group provide carbohydrates, vitamins, minerals and fibre. Aim to eat at least one food from this group at every meal and at least six servings each day.

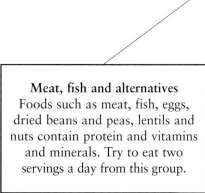

Meat, fish and alternatives
Foods such as meat, fish, eggs, dried beans and peas, lentils and nuts contain protein and vitamins and minerals. Try to eat two servings a day from this group.

Fatty and sugary foods
The fifth group of foods includes things such as biscuits, doughnuts, crisps, corn snacks, ice cream, mayonnaise, bottled sauces, honey, sweets, chocolate and sweet drinks. Because these foods contain a lot of calories but relatively few nutrients, it is best not to eat them very often, and even then only in small amounts.

Milk and dairy foods
These foods, such as yoghurt and cheese, provide protein, calcium and other vitamins and minerals. You should eat three servings from this group every day.

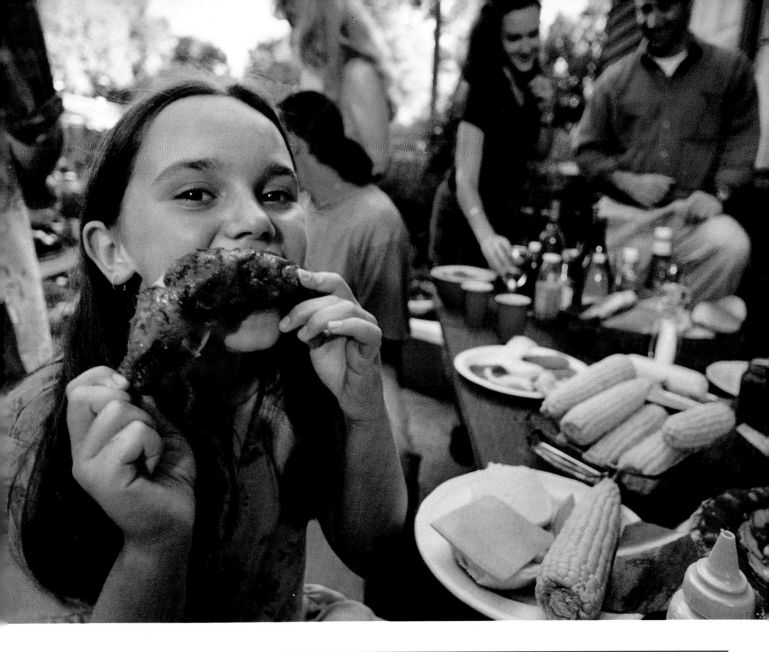

Many different foods can provide the nutrients you need – the important thing is to make sure you enjoy what you eat.

By following these guidelines and making sure you have a good breakfast, lunch and dinner each day, you should get a healthy, balanced diet. You can also eat two or three small snacks a day – just be sure that they are healthy ones and not 'junk food'. The food plate opposite illustrates the basic principles of a healthy diet.

DIETARY DOS AND DON'TS

Do
★ Enjoy your food.
★ Eat a variety of different foods.
★ Eat sufficient food to keep you at a healthy weight.
★ Eat plenty of foods rich in starch and fibre.
★ Eat plenty of fruit and vegetables.

Don't
★ Eat too many foods that contain a lot of fat.
★ Consume sugary foods and drinks too often.

FOOD IS FOR GROWTH

A good diet is crucial as you enter your teens, when you are growing taller and heavier and need extra energy and nutrients. Eating protein foods such as meat, fish, lentils and beans helps your muscles grow and develop. Calcium, found in milk, cheese and yoghurt, is necessary for your bones to grow strong and healthy. Iron from meat, oily fish and lentils is also vital. Red blood cells contain lots of iron, and the amount of blood in your body is constantly increasing as you grow. Iron is especially important for girls once they start having periods.

GROWTH RATES IN BOYS AND GIRLS

The growth spurt – the sudden surge in height and weight that happens during your teens – starts around age ten in girls and twelve in boys. The make-up of your body changes too. Girls put on more fat and boys lose fat. These differences mean that boys and girls need different amounts of food. If you eat according to your appetite you will generally get enough nutrients and calories, provided you make healthy choices. To make sure you are eating the right amount, ask your doctor to check your height- and weight-gain from time to time against a growth chart.

Above The rapid increase in growth during your teens means that your energy and nutrient needs increase.

Right On these growth charts, the darker blue areas between the red lines show the range of normal weight and height at different ages. The green line in the middle shows the average height or weight. At any one age, about 50 per cent of children will be above the line, and about 50 per cent below it. If you measure your height and weight regularly and mark the measurements on the charts, you will get a line that shows your own growth line. Your line should run parallel to the green line. If it does not, or if it is above or below the red lines, you should consult a doctor.

DID YOU KNOW?

★ Up to the age of ten, your body consists of about 18 per cent fat. During adolescence girls' body fat increases to about 28 per cent and boys' decreases to about 15 per cent.

★ Your body uses around 100 calories a day simply to grow.

★ Between eleven and fourteen, you need about 2,220 calories a day if you are boy and around 1,845 calories if you are a girl.

★ During the growth spurt you can expect to grow an average of 23 centimetres taller and put on 20–26 kilograms in weight.

BOY'S HEIGHT CHART

GIRL'S HEIGHT CHART

BOY'S WEIGHT CHART

GIRL'S WEIGHT CHART

11

ENERGY

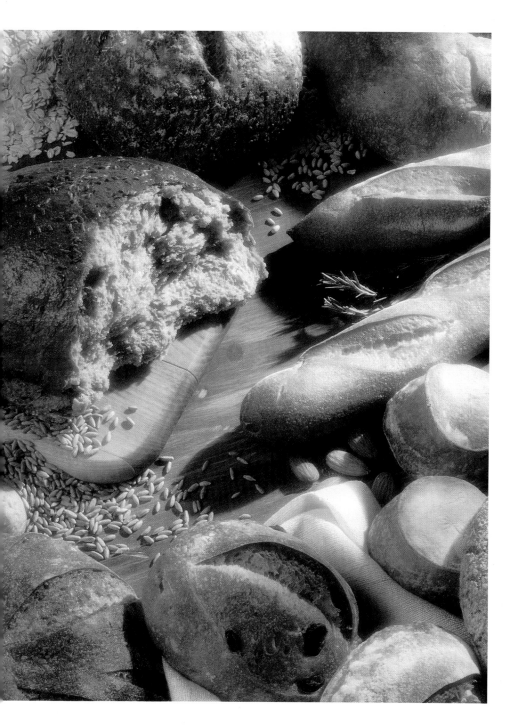

All types of bread contain starch, which your body breaks down to get energy.

CARBOHYDRATES

The main source of fuel for your body is a group of foods known as carbohydrates. Chemical reactions inside your body break down carbohydrates, releasing energy for your body to use. There are three main types of carbohydrate: starch, fibre and sugar.

STARCH FOR STAMINA

Starch is found in bread, pasta, rice, cassava, potatoes, yams and other foods. It is known as a complex carbohydrate. Your body breaks down starch very slowly, gradually releasing the energy it contains over several hours. This keeps your energy levels stable and gives you the stamina to keep going.

WHY YOU NEED FIBRE

Fibre is also a complex carbohydrate. Your body does not fully digest fibre, but the fibre plays an important part in keeping you healthy. Insoluble fibre, sometimes called roughage, is found in bran (the husks of whole-grain cereals such as brown rice) and in the skin and seeds of fruits, vegetables, beans and nuts.

TRUE OR FALSE?

An apple a day keeps the doctor away.
True. Most fruit and vegetables contain soluble and insoluble fibre. Apple peel is made up an insoluble fibre called cellulose, while apple flesh is a source of a soluble fibre called pectin. Apples also contain vitamins and minerals that help protect you against disease.

Insoluble fibre helps to prevent constipation and enables waste products from food to pass smoothly through your digestive system. It also reduces your chances of developing bowel disease.

Rice is the main source of carbohydrate for people in some parts of the world.

SOLUBLE FIBRE

A second type of fibre, called soluble fibre, is partly broken down by the digestive system. It is found in beans, lentils, most fruit and vegetables, porridge oats, rye bread and barley. It helps to lower levels of cholesterol, a substance that contributes to heart disease, and prevent sudden increases in blood sugar, which can lead to uneven energy levels. To make sure you get the right amount of fibre – both soluble and insoluble – eat a variety of different fibre-rich foods each day, rather than just sprinkling bran on your cereal.

TYPES OF SUGAR

Sugar is a simple carbohydrate, which means that your body can break it down quickly. There are many different types of sugar. Sucrose is a type of sugar used in sweets, biscuits, cakes and soft drinks. Other sugars include fructose (found in fruit and honey), glucose (honey, fruit and vegetables), maltose (sprouting grains) and lactose (milk). They all give you energy, but only glucose is immediately available for your body to use. Other types of sugars must first be converted to glucose inside your body.

WHY TOO MANY SWEETS ARE BAD FOR YOU

Sugar, the main ingredient of sweets, can cause tooth decay. Although sweets are crammed full of energy – about 375 calories per 100 grams – they contain few important vitamins and minerals. Sweets are digested quickly, causing a rapid rise in your blood-sugar levels and giving you a quick burst of energy. Unfortunately, it doesn't last long, and you soon feel tired and lacklustre. Sweets can also dent your appetite for more nutritious food. Last but not least, many sweets contain artificial colourings that cause allergic reactions such as wheezing, headaches and rashes in some people.

DOES CHOCOLATE MAKE YOU SPOTTY?

It is a myth that chocolate makes you spotty. Spots and blackheads (acne) are mainly due to the hormonal changes that occur during adolescence. In fact, chocolate is one of the best sweets to eat, and less liable to cause tooth decay than others. It contains some protein and minerals, as well as substances that are said to boost brain chemicals and help you to feel good. It also contains caffeine, which makes you more alert. Now for the bad news: chocolate is very high in fat and calories, so it can make you put on weight. As with other sweets, it is best eaten only as a treat.

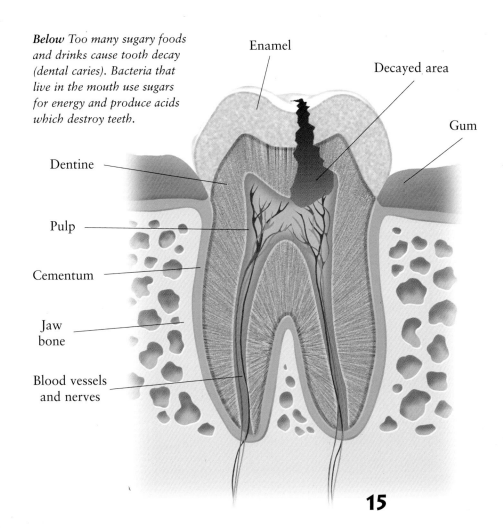

Below *Too many sugary foods and drinks cause tooth decay (dental caries). Bacteria that live in the mouth use sugars for energy and produce acids which destroy teeth.*

Enamel

Decayed area

Gum

Dentine

Pulp

Cementum

Jaw bone

Blood vessels and nerves

TRUE OR FALSE?

Eating a banana can improve your tennis. True. Eating a banana won't improve your serve, but it can help give you the energy to win the match. Bananas contain both sugar and starch. This means that they give you instant energy as well as sustaining your energy level over a longer period of time.

PROTEIN

WHAT IS PROTEIN FOR?

You need protein for your body's growth, maintenance, and repair. Protein helps to you have strong muscles and fight off infections. It also strengthens your hormonal system. The precise amount of protein you need varies, but if you eat a balanced diet you should get all you need. Any extra protein that you take in but do not use up will be burned inside your body to provide energy or transformed into fat.

Below All types of fish are good sources of protein and other vital nutrients. White fish are low in fat, while oily fish provide Omega-3 fats, which research shows can help to prevent heart disease.

AMINO ACIDS

Protein is one of the most complicated substances in the human body. When you digest protein, it is broken down into much simpler substances called amino acids. Your body uses these to repair muscle, skin and other tissues and to build a strong immune system. Some of the 20 amino acids found in protein can be manufactured by your body, but eight – called essential amino acids – can only be obtained from food.

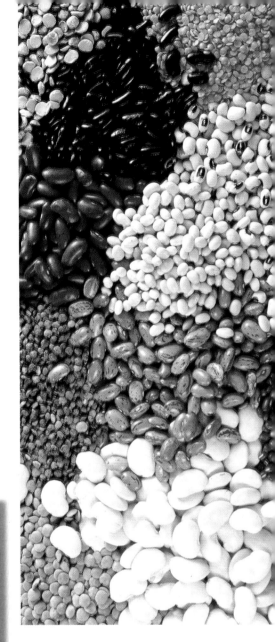

Above Shellfish, including prawns, crabs and lobsters, are rich in essential amino acids, which cannot be manufactured by your body.

Right Beans, lentils, chickpeas and other types of peas and beans provide protein, but they do not contain enough of all the essential amino acids.

PROTEIN SUPPORT

Protein supports your body's structure by forming part of muscles, bones, cartilages, and teeth. But it can also be a source of energy too. If you do not eat enough food to give you sufficient energy – such as during a period of fasting (eating no food for religious reasons) – amino acids can be converted to sugar in your blood to provide you with energy.

TYPES OF PROTEIN

Meat, fish, shellfish, eggs, dairy products and soya products (such as soya milk, soya beans and tofu) contain all eight of the essential amino acids. Such foods are known as high-quality proteins. Cereals, beans (except soya beans), lentils and nuts are proteins, but they do not contain all the essential amino acids. That is why they often are called low-quality proteins.

GETTING ENOUGH PROTEIN

If you eat meat and fish it is easy to get all the amino acids you need because your diet automatically includes high-quality proteins.

Vegetarians who do not always eat soya products should eat a variety of different plant foods to get the right amount of protein. When you eat low-quality proteins together – for example baked beans on toast, rice and dhal (lentil curry), rice and peas, or a peanut butter sandwich – the amino acids in them combine to provide you with similar protein levels to those found in meat. This is known as complementary eating. So if you are vegetarian, provided you eat a varied, balanced diet you won't go short of protein.

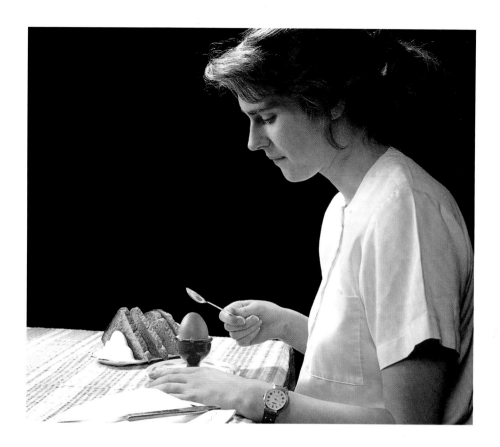

Many vegetarians get their high-quality protein from eggs and soya products.

SOURCES OF PROTEINS

MEAT AND FISH EATERS	VEGETARIANS
Chicken	Baked beans
Turkey	Haricot beans
Pheasant	Soya beans and soya
Rabbit	products (e.g. tofu, miso,
Ham	soya milk)
Beef	Broad beans
Pork	Aduki beans
Lamb	Butter beans
Salmon	Hazel nuts
Trout	Cashew nuts
Cod	Brazil nuts
Tuna	Cheese
Swordfish	Eggs

DO ATHLETES NEED EXTRA PROTEIN?

It is sometimes said that athletes need extra protein. True, muscle is mostly made of protein, but excess protein can reduce the water content of body tissues and harm athletic performance. What athletes really need is carbohydrates for extra energy. Body-builders are different. They do need extra protein to help build muscle tissue. Body-builders tend to eat more than the average person, so they naturally take in more protein. Their needs can be met by a healthy, balanced diet, without need to take protein or amino acid tablets.

If you are an athlete, you should eat plenty of starchy carbohydrate foods – rather than extra protein – to give your muscles the fuel they need to make you a winner.

FAT

THE PROS AND CONS OF FATS

Fat is the most concentrated source of energy in your diet. It provides you with twice as many calories as carbohydrate or protein. Fats help your food taste better, give it a better texture and give it flavour and smell. Some kinds of fats contain nutrients that you need for growth and the development of tissues such as those in your brain. The layer of fat under your skin also helps you to keep warm. You need to eat some fats and oils, but eating too many of the wrong kind can make you overweight.

FATS TO EAT MORE OF

Make sure your diet contains plenty of fish, vegetables, seeds, nuts and dress your salad with oils such as olive, soya, or sesame.

Below Fish and chips provides protein, carbohydrate and fat – but don't eat them too often, as they are high in saturated fat.

A FISHY STORY

Oily fish, such as mackerel, herring, tuna and salmon, contain a group of fatty acids called Omega-3. These fats help the brain and eyes to develop in unborn and newborn babies. Omega-3 fats also help to reduce inflammation and the tendency of blood to clot. They can be used to treat heart disease, the skin complaint psoriasis and arthritis. Omega-3 fats are also found in walnuts and rapeseed oil.

Above These are fat cells, magnified 750 times. They accumulate in a thick layer under your skin that helps to keep you warm and acts as an energy store.

This will ensure that you get enough of the healthiest types of fats called unsaturated fats. You need unsaturated fats to provide you with a group of nutrients called essential fatty acids.

FATS TO EAT LESS OF

Fats that tend to be hard at room temperature, such as butter, meat fat, lard and cheese, are called saturated fats. They mainly come from animals and animal products. Eating too many of these can increase the risk of heart disease.

To ensure you do not get an excess of saturated fats, avoid eating too many fried foods. Choose lean cuts of meat and eat more poultry, such as chicken and turkey, which are lower in saturated fats than red meats.

FATS TO EAT IN MODERATION

Biscuits, pies, cakes, crisps, fatty sauces and mayonnaise contain trans fats. These fats, created by food processing, may also be a risk factor for heart disease, so it is wise to avoid eating too many foods containing them.

VITAMINS AND MINERALS

ESSENTIAL SUBSTANCES

The chemical processes that keep your body going rely heavily on vitamins and minerals. Although your body only needs them in small amounts and they do not provide you with energy, vitamins and minerals are still absolutely essential. Fruit and vegetables are especially rich in these substances.

Below A market stall in Malaysia. Fresh fruit and vegetables contain more vitamins and minerals than most manufactured or processed foods.

WHAT DO VITAMINS AND MINERALS DO?

Each vitamin or mineral has its own specific job. For example, vitamin A is good for your eyesight, vitamin C helps you fight infections and the mineral iron helps you to have healthy blood. As well performing important jobs on their own, vitamins and minerals also work alongside each other. Vitamin C, for example, helps the body to absorb and use iron.

WHY SHOULD YOU EAT UP YOUR GREENS?

Green vegetables such as broccoli, cabbage, lettuce and spinach contain many important vitamins and minerals. They are especially rich in vitamin C. Dark-green leafy vegetables also contain a B vitamin called folic acid, which your body needs to produce new cells. A shortage of folic acid can cause anaemia. Try to eat at least a portion of these every day.

Above Green leafy vegetables, such as this lettuce, are a good source of vitamin C and the mineral folic acid.

DID YOU KNOW?

★ Smoking increases the need for vitamin C. People who smoke should increase their daily intake of vitamin C by drinking an extra glass of fresh orange juice each day.

WATER-SOLUBLE VITAMINS

Some vitamins, such as the C and B group vitamins, are called water-soluble vitamins because they dissolve in water. Because you are constantly losing water through sweat and urine, your body cannot store water-soluble vitamins. This means that you need to eat foods containing them every day. Unfortunately, we sometimes ruin these vitamins in the process of cooking food. Boiling vegetables for too long can destroy water-soluble vitamins, so steaming vegetables is better. To be sure of obtaining these vitamins, it is a good idea to eat some vegetables raw in salads.

Salads are an important part of a healthy, balanced diet, because the raw vegetables they contain are especially rich in vitamins and minerals.

VITAL VITAMINS

VITAMIN	WHY YOU NEED IT	WHERE TO FIND IT
A	Growth	Tuna, herring, mackerel, liver, kidneys, milk, eggs, cheese, margarine, butter
Beta-carotene	May help fight against certain kinds of cancer	Carrots, broccoli, spinach, cabbage, oranges, tomatoes, red and yellow peppers, pumpkins, squash, sweet potatoes, cantaloupe and ogen melons
B group vitamins	Growth and development, healthy nervous system, digestion, converting food into energy	Liver, yeast extract, meat, milk, yoghurt, cheese, butter, eggs, fish, whole-grain cereals, dark green vegetables, Brazil nuts, pistachio nuts, walnuts, beans, bananas
C	Healthy teeth, bones, skin; helps absorb iron	Fruit and vegetables such as peppers, citrus fruits, strawberries, blackcurrants, potatoes
D	Helps body absorb calcium and phosphorus for healthy bones and teeth	Fish liver oils, eggs, fortified margarines, tuna, salmon, sardines
E	Helps protect against heart disease	Vegetable oils, nuts, seeds, margarine
K	Needed for normal blood clotting	Green leafy vegetables, especially cabbage, broccoli, Brussels sprouts

FAT-SOLUBLE VITAMINS

Vitamins such as A, D, E, K and beta-carotene dissolve in fat in your body and are stored in your liver and other places. Because they are fat-soluble, your body absorbs them better if you eat a bit of fat at the same time as you take in the vitamins. Having carrots (which contain beta-carotene) as part of a meal that is cooked with a dash of oil will help to make your body more efficient at absorbing these vitamins.

VITAMIN DEFICIENCIES

If your body does not get enough of a particular vitamin from your diet, you may develop a deficiency disease. A severe lack of vitamin C, for example, results in scurvy, a deficiency disease that causes swollen joints and internal bleeding. Sailors used to suffer from scurvy because they could not get enough fresh food on long voyages. In developing countries, deficiency of vitamin A is linked to childhood blindness.

A dermatologist looks at a woman's face through a lens to examine a skin complaint. Vitamin C, found in most fruit and vegetables, is particularly important for healthy skin.

WHAT ARE MINERALS?

You need minerals to enable your body to perform hundreds of vital processes. Some minerals become part of your bones, teeth and muscles, and some are needed for chemical reactions in your body. Other minerals help to balance your body's fluid levels and regulate the acidity of your blood. Two of the most important minerals during your teenage years are iron and calcium.

HOW IS IRON IMPORTANT?

Iron is an essential part of haemoglobin, a protein found in red blood cells. Haemoglobin carries oxygen around your body and releases it wherever it is needed. There are two types of iron: one type is found in meat, fish and poultry, while the other occurs in non-meat foods such as dark-green vegetables, dried fruits such as apricots, fortified cereals and breads.

Above Disc-shaped red blood cells passing through a vein. Iron is important for the formation of haemoglobin, the oxygen-carrying protein found in red blood cells.

ABSORBING IRON

Non-meat iron is the hardest type for your body to absorb. Vitamin C helps us absorb it, so eating an orange or drinking a glass of fresh orange juice with meals containing iron is helpful. Other substances such as tannins, which are found in tea, can block iron absorption by as much as half, so try not to drink tea with an iron-containing meal.

MINERAL DEFICIENCIES

Like vitamins, minerals are vital to the proper functioning of our bodies, so a diet that is lacking in a certain mineral can cause a deficiency disease. If your body is not getting enough iron, for example, you could develop anaemia, a blood disease in which people look pale and become tired very easily.

Below Eating plenty of vitamin-C-rich fresh fruit will help your body to absorb the essential mineral iron from non-meat sources, such as dark-green vegetables and cereals.

WHERE DOES CALCIUM COME FROM?

Milk and dairy foods are
especially rich in calcium. Having
three servings a day will meet your
needs. A serving is a glass of milk,
a small pot of yoghurt or a
matchbox-sized piece of cheese.
Although calcium is also found in
bread, beans, tinned fish with
bones, nuts, seeds, dried fruit and
green leafy vegetables, it is
sometimes poorly absorbed.
Eating foods containing vitamin
D, such as oily fish, margarine,
eggs and fortified breakfast cereals
will help your body absorb
calcium from these sources.

*Shellfish are a good source of iodine –
a key mineral for healthy growth.*

OTHER IMPORTANT MINERALS

Apart from iron and calcium,
other minerals that are
particularly important when your
body is growing are magnesium,
phosphorous and iodine. Zinc also
is also important for growth and
sexual development.

*Milk is an especially good source of
calcium, which your body needs for
strong bones and healthy teeth.*

MINERAL MAGIC

Mineral	Why you need it	Where to find it
Calcium	Healthy bones and teeth, helping messages pass between nerves, blood clotting, muscle, function	Milk and dairy foods, tinned sardines, nuts, sesame seeds, broccoli
Chloride	Helps maintain body's fluid balance; too much is linked to high blood-pressure	Table salt (sodium chloride), packet soups, stock cubes, processed foods, ready meals, snacks such as crisps
Fluorine	Healthy teeth and bones	Seafood, sea salt, tap water
Iodine	Healthy thyroid gland (the thyroid is involved in growth and controls energy-release in the body)	Seafood, seaweed
Iron	Healthy blood, especially red blood cells	Liver, kidneys, sardines, dark green vegetables, apricots, breakfast cereals
Magnesium	Healthy bones and teeth, healthy nerves, helps muscles contract	Whole-grain cereals, nuts, dried peas and beans, sesame seeds, dried figs, green vegetables
Phosphorus	Healthy bones and teeth, helps release energy from cells, helps absorb other nutrients	Milk, cheese, meat, fish, poultry, cheese, nuts, seeds, cereals
Potassium	Helps maintain fluid balance, keeps heartbeat, regular and maintains blood pressure	Bananas, avocado pears, potatoes, seeds, nuts
Zinc	Growth, sexual development, healthy immune system	Oysters, red meat, peanuts, sunflower seeds

FOOD SUPPLEMENTS

If you are not getting enough nutrients from your diet, you can take 'food supplements', which are vitamins and minerals in pill, capsule or liquid form. For example, if you are not eating a well-balanced diet because you are on a strict slimming regime, you could be depriving yourself of essential nutrients and may benefit from a supplement containing a balanced range of vitamins and minerals. If you are severely anaemic, your doctor may prescribe a supplement of iron and vitamin C.

SUPPLEMENTS FOR VEGANS

If you eat no animal products because you are vegan, you may need a vitamin B 12 supplement, which is only found naturally in foods of animal origin. You may also need a calcium supplement, as the body does not absorb calcium very well from non-animal sources.

KEEPING YOURSELF WELL

Some nutritional experts believe that taking vitamin or mineral supplements in addition to a healthy diet can protect against certain diseases. Extra vitamin E, for example, may protect against the risk of heart disease.

SUPPLEMENT DANGERS

Some vitamin and mineral supplements are dangerous in excess. Your body cannot get rid of fat-soluble vitamins such as vitamins A and D. Too much vitamin A can damage the liver and bones and cause abnormalities in an unborn baby, while an excess of vitamin D can cause calcium to build up and damage the heart and kidneys.

Above Vitamin and mineral supplements can help if you are not getting enough nutrients from your diet. However, taking too many supplements can be dangerous.

Right Under normal circumstances, a healthy diet and plenty of energetic activity should provide you with all the strength and stamina you need, without having to take supplements.

CAN SUPPLEMENTS BUILD MUSCLES?

Adverts for 'high-performance' sports drinks and foods often claim that they boost your strength and muscles. Some of these products contain large doses of amino acids or vitamins and minerals. But such supplements are not helpful, and may even be harmful. The best way develop muscles is to exercise regularly and eat a well-balanced, high-carbohydrate, low-fat diet.

HEALTHY EATING FOR LIFE

FOOD AND ILLNESS

Doctors have known for some time that people eating a diet containing lots of fatty foods run a greater risk of becoming overweight and developing high blood-pressure and heart disease. In the last few years, it has also been discovered that many vitamins, minerals and other substances in food can actively protect your body against illness and disease.

VITAMINS ARE ACE!

The vitamins beta-carotene, C and E are often known as the ACE vitamins. The 'A' in ACE refers to the fact that your body converts beta-carotene into vitamin A. Together, the ACE vitamins are antioxidants. This means that they help to keep your cells healthy by mopping up substances called free radicals, which can damage your cells. Free-radical damage is linked to diseases such as heart disease, cancer, arthritis, diabetes and cataracts (when the lenses of the eyes become cloudy).

FOOD AS MEDICINE?

Long before people knew about vitamins and minerals, doctors used food and herbs to treat illnesses. Scientists have now begun to identify a whole range of plant chemicals in food that act like medicines and help you to fight serious illnesses such as heart disease and cancer.

This X-ray image shows the hands of a person with rheumatoid arthritis. Some doctors and scientists think that allergy to some foods may be a factor in rheumatoid arthritis.

This man is making up a Chinese herbal treatment, which uses phytochemicals to prevent and treat disease.

These substances are called phytochemicals. They include allium compounds in onions, garlic and chives, flavonoids in most fruit, vegetables, tea and red wine, limonene found in oranges, lemons and grapefruit, and diothiolthiones found in broccoli, Brussels sprouts, cabbage and cauliflower.

DID YOU KNOW?

★ Levels of heart disease and cancer are very low in Italy, Spain, Greece and other countries around the Mediterranean Sea. This is because they eat a very healthy diet containing lots of fruit and vegetables, a little fish, lean meat, olive oil and a small amount of wine.

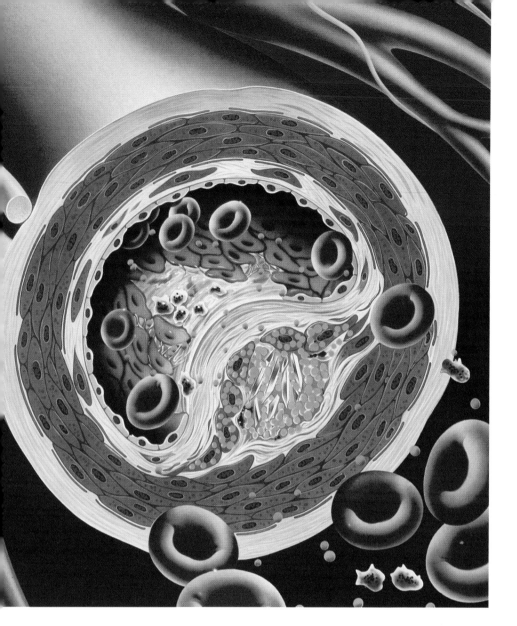

In heart disease, large blood vessels called arteries become clogged with a waxy, fatty substance called cholesterol (coloured yellow in the picture). Consuming too many saturated and trans fats can raise cholesterol levels.

DIABETES

If you have diabetes, the pancreas gland in your body does not make enough insulin. Insulin is a substance that controls your body's blood-sugar levels. Some people with diabetes have to inject themselves with insulin, but the food they eat is also very important in making sure that their blood-sugar levels do not go too high or too low. People with diabetes need a diet that is high in complex carbohdyrates and fibre, and low in sugar and fat.

HEART DISEASE

For a healthy heart you should eat plenty of fruit and vegetables. They are rich in vitamins that help stop blood vessels called arteries from clogging up with cholesterol, which is one of the causes of heart attacks. Butter, cream, fatty meats and foods high in saturated and trans fats also raise cholesterol levels, so keep them to a minimum. Being overweight increases the risk of heart disease, so eat a healthy, low-fat diet and take enough exercise to stay a healthy weight.

PROTECTION AGAINST CANCER

Cancer is a serious disease that occurs when some of the cells in your body divide and grow faster than they should. Experts think that eating properly can protect you against some kinds of cancer.

Make sure your diet gives you plenty of ACE vitamins and fibre. Avoid eating too many animal fats and go easy on foods like bacon, salami and smoked meats. They are preserved with substances that have been linked to stomach cancer. Try not to eat barbecued food. Burning can produce harmful substances that could cause cancer.

THE ORGANIC OPTION

Many chemicals are sprayed on farm crops, including fertilizers to help them grow and pesticides to stop insects eating them. It is not known if these chemicals cause cancer, but many experts believe it is healthier to eat organic food, which is produced without the use of such chemicals.

Barbecued foods contain high levels of chemicals produced by burning that have been linked to bowel and other forms of cancer.

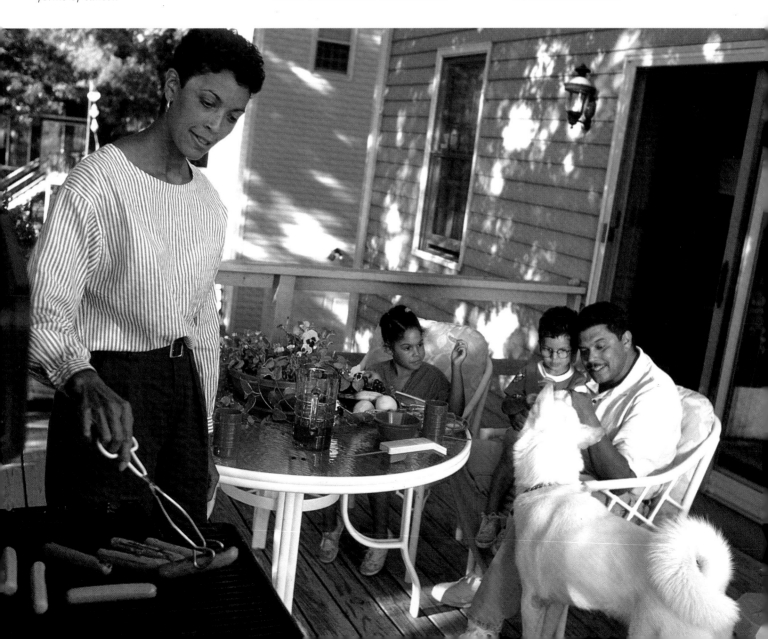

VEGETARIANISM

If you are vegetarian you do not eat meat, poultry, game, fish or animal products such as gelatine and lard. Most vegetarians eat cheese, milk, yoghurt and eggs that are produced by animals. Vegans are vegetarians who avoid all animal products.

WHY BE VEGETARIAN?

People are vegetarian for many different reasons, perhaps because they are worried about cruelty to animals, or because their religion forbids them to eat meat. Others are vegetarian simply because they do not like the taste of meat. Many people choose a vegetarian diet because they believe that avoiding meat and meat products is better for their health.

GOOD HEALTH WITHOUT MEAT

A well-balanced, low-saturated-fat, high-fibre vegetarian diet is extremely healthy. Vegetarians have a lower risk of certain cancers, heart disease and conditions such as kidney- and gall-stones than non-vegetarians.

They also have less chance of developing diabetes and high blood-pressure, and are less likely to be overweight. Provided you eat a variety of foods, including grains and cereals, fruit and vegetables, beans and peas, nuts, seeds and a small amount of fat, you will get all the nutrients you need – whether or not you consume animal products.

MEETING SPECIAL NEEDS

Vitamin B 12, an essential nutrient, is only found in animal foods. If you are vegan you will not get any in your diet. You can meet your body's need for B12 by eating margarine and other foods fortified with B 12 (that is, with B 12 specially added). Alternatively, you can take a vitamin B 12 supplement. Calcium is important when you are growing, so if you are vegetarian you should make sure you eat at least three servings of dairy foods or foods fortified with vitamin D and calcium. every day.

Left Lacto-vegetarians avoid meat and meat products, poultry and fish, but include dairy products such as cheese and yoghurt in their diet. Vegans, by contrast, avoid all foods containing animal products.

Right A tasty vegetarian meal of pasta, vegetables and herbs. A well-balanced vegetarian diet can provide you with all the nutrients you need for good health.

The occasional cheeseburger will not do you any harm, but avoid eating too many, as they are high in sugar and fat.

SNACKING AND GRAZING

When your parents were children, they probably sat down to three 'proper' meals a day. Today, eating habits are much more casual. Instead of eating breakfast, lunch and dinner you may eat on and off throughout the day, a style of eating often called grazing or snacking. When you feel peckish or thirsty, you grab a snack or help yourself to a drink. The availability of fast foods, ready meals and packet snacks makes it easier to graze.

WHY AVOID TOO MUCH JUNK FOOD?

Snacking is not a bad way to eat, as long as you choose nutritious snacks. But snacks from vending machines and fast-food restaurants are often 'junk foods' – high in fats and sugars and low in vitamins and minerals. They are also high in sodium, which is found in salt. Too much sodium can cause a rise in blood pressure, which in turn is linked to heart disease.

A LITTLE OF WHAT YOU FANCY

Junk and fast foods are fine from time to time, but try not to eat too many. A baked potato topped by baked beans with salad and fruit juice is healthier than a cheeseburger, chips and a bottle of pop. Popcorn (with no butter or salt) is healthier than packet snacks such as crisps. Look at the back of packets to see what they contain. Choose those with the least fat, sugar and salt.

CHOOSE THE HEALTHY OPTION

In a fast-food restaurant or school cafeteria think before you order. Choose a balanced meal containing carbohydrate, protein and vegetables. Think about the way the food is cooked – grilled or baked foods are better for you than fried foods.

FOOD	CHOOSE	LIMIT
Fish	Grilled or baked	Deep fried and battered
Chicken	Skinless and grilled	Deep fried and coated
Pizza	Vegetable toppings such as mushrooms, pepper, spinach, aubergine	Fatty toppings such as sausage, bacon, or extra cheese
Vegetables and salads	Fresh, eaten raw or steamed	Creamy, fatty dressings and sauces such as salad cream mayonnaise, blue cheese
Potatoes	Baked	Fried skins, chips
Drinks	Juice, water, low-fat milk shakes small sizes	Full-fat milk shakes, squashes, sweet fizzy drinks large sizes
Puddings	Fresh fruit, yoghurt fruit salad	Doughnuts, fried apple pie, chocolate fudge cake, banoffee pie

When helping yourself to a snack, make sure you choose something healthy.

Below Lack of activity combined with too many unhealthy snacks can make you put on more weight than is healthy.

WEIGHT-WATCHING

Being overweight makes it harder for you to run around. It may also make you short of breath and can put a strain on your joints. Adults who are overweight, or obese, are more likely to develop diabetes, high blood-pressure and heart disease. Obese women are more likely to develop breast cancer.

ARE YOU OVERWEIGHT?

Doctors use what is called a body-mass index (BMI) chart to check if people are overweight. If you are concerned that you may be overweight, consult your doctor. You may have a high BMI if you are very muscular because you exercise a lot. In this case, you are not overweight.

WHY DO YOU GAIN WEIGHT?

You may inherit the tendency to gain weight from your parents through your genes. Your genes can affect when you feel full, where your body stores fat and how fast you burn energy. Body weight is also linked to eating habits and exercise levels. People often overeat if they are sad, angry or bored. You are more likely to put on weight if you sit around a lot watching television.

ACHIEVING A HEALTHY WEIGHT

If you are overweight, make sure you eat a well-balanced diet. If you currently do little or no exercise, initially aim for at least 30 minutes exercise each day, such as walking or cycling, and gradually build up your activity level as you get fitter.

CONTROLLING YOUR WEIGHT

At least twice a week, try to do some more vigorous exercise such as running, dancing, tennis or swimming. As you are growing it is usually best to aim to maintain the same weight rather than actually trying to lose it.

DID YOU KNOW?

★ Some adults are 'apple shaped', which means that they store fat around their middle.
★ Others are 'pear shaped' and store fat around their hips and thighs.
★ Apple-shaped people are more likely to develop heart disease than pear-shaped people.

ARE YOU UNDERWEIGHT?

If you are naturally thin and wiry you are probably perfectly healthy. However, if you do not weigh as much as you should because you have been severely cutting down on food, you could damage your health. Rapid, unexplained weight loss can be a sign of illness. Eating a balanced diet will ensure that you maintain a healthy weight.

If you eat well and exercise regularly you will have plenty of energy and be the right weight for your age and height.

WHAT ARE EATING DISORDERS?

Eating disorders affect the way you think about food and what you eat. People with them are obsessed with what they look like, especially what they weigh. People with anorexia nervosa deliberately do not eat enough and become severely underweight. Often they imagine they are fatter than they are. They feel so ashamed of the way they look they often avoid doing things like gym or swimming where they have to reveal their bodies.

Eating disorders may develop as a way of coping with problems. They can often be overcome with a counsellor's help.

BINGE EATING

People with bulimia nervosa usually weigh the right amount but have no control over what they eat. They eat huge amounts in a short time. This is called a binge. It causes them to feel so bad that they make themselves sick. Sometimes they take laxatives (drugs that make you empty your bowels) or starve themselves to make up for bingeing.

COPING WITH EATING DISORDERS

If you have an eating disorder you need to find out what your correct weight should be and learn to eat healthily. You will also need the help and advice of an expert such as a doctor, dietitian or counsellor.

DIETARY TRAFFIC-LIGHTS

STOP
Fatty and sugary foods to be limited
Fatty and fried foods: butter, margarine, lard, crisps, chips, fried vegetables, cream.
Sugary foods: jam, marmalade, honey, syrup, sweets, chocolates, toffee, ice cream, cakes, biscuits, puddings, pies and pastries, sweet drinks.

STEADY
Needed in moderate amounts for growth
Protein foods: lean meat, fish, eggs, cheese, baked beans, dried peas and beans, nuts.
Milk: skimmed or semi-skimmed.
Cereals: bread, cereal, pasta, rice.

Go
Nutritious foods to fill up on
Vegetables: raw, boiled, steamed, in salads.
Fruit: fresh, frozen, canned in juice.
Drinks: tea, coffee, water.
Seasonings: herbs, spices.

FOOD ALLERGIES

If eating a certain food frequently makes you have a rash, wheezing or sneezing, a headache, swelling or an upset stomach, you could have an allergy or a food intolerance. An allergy happens when your immune system, which protects you against disease, reacts to a substance that is normally harmless to your body. With a food intolerance, your body reacts to something you eat but the reaction does not involve your immune system.

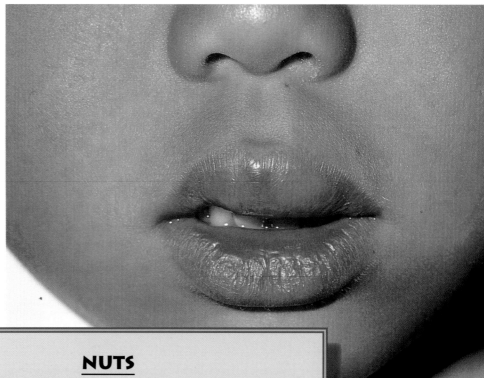

Below Peanuts are one of the most common causes of food allergy. Peanut oil is often used to make foods such as biscuits, cakes and puddings.

NUTS

Some people are allergic to nuts, especially peanuts, walnuts and cashew nuts. Eating even a small amount of nut, such as a biscuit made with peanut oil, can cause their tongues, lips and throats to swell up or bring on a severe asthma attack. Sometimes the reaction is so severe the person goes into a serious kind of shock, called anaphylactic shock, and may die. People who are at risk carry a phial containing a hormone called adrenaline, which can stop the reaction.

Above This boy's swollen upper lip is caused by an allergic reaction to eating peanuts.

ALLERGIES IN CHILDREN

People of all ages are affected by allergies, but they are particularly common in childhood. You may be among the one in three children who have an allergy such as asthma, eczema, hayfever or urticaria (a red, raised rash sometimes called nettle rash). Foods are one cause of allergies. The main culprits are milk and dairy products, wheat, eggs, shellfish, nuts, soya beans and some additives and colourings found in processed foods.

AVOIDING ALLERGIES

If you think you are allergic to something you eat, the doctor can do a test to check which food may be causing the trouble. He or she may then advise you to stop eating that food altogether. After a time, you may be able to reintroduce small amounts of the food into your diet. You should only exclude a particular food or type of food from your diet if you are advised to do so by your doctor or a dietitian.

ALLERGY-CAUSING FOODS

FOOD	POSSIBLE SYMPTOMS
Milk and dairy products such as milk, butter, ice cream, cheese, yoghurt	Diarrhoea, constipation, migraine (a type of headache), pain in the abdomen, eczema
Gluten found in flour, and bread, biscuits, tinned and packet soups, stock cubes and processed foods	Migraine and coeliac disease, which causes diarrhoea, weight-loss and anaemia
Eggs, usually the white part used in cakes, meringues, mayonnaise and ice cream	Rashes, swelling, stomach upsets, asthma, eczema
Shellfish such as prawns, shrimps, crabs and mussels	Stomach aches, migraine, nausea (feeling sick)
Nuts, especially peanuts, walnuts, cashews; also in nut bread, biscuits and sweets, ice cream and oils	Rashes, swelling, asthma, eczema. In severe cases, anaphylactic shock
Some additives, colourings and flavourings found in processed foods	Wheezing and other allergic reactions; some experts believe they may cause hyperactivity, behaviour and learning difficulties

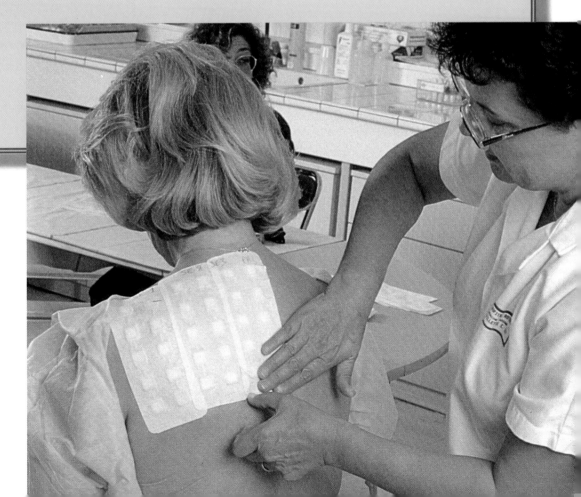

This woman is having a patch test to identify exactly what is the cause of her allergy. Small amounts of different substances are applied to her skin to see if they produce mildly allergic reactions. Food allergies are usually tested by omitting certain foods from a person's diet.

GLOSSARY

Allergy A reaction by your immune system to food or other usually harmless substances such as pollen, dust, feathers or fur.

Amino acids The building blocks of proteins. There are about 20 amino acids, which join together to make many different proteins.

Anaemia A condition in which the blood's level of haemoglobin – a type of protein that carries oxygen – is low. This reduces the supply of oxygen to the body's tissues.

Antioxidant A substance or nutrient that mops up free radicals, making them harmless. Vitamins A, C, E and the minerals iron, zinc, copper, manganese and selenium are antioxidants.

Carbohydrate A type of major nutrient needed by the body for energy. Simple carbohydrates have small molecules, while complex carbohydrates have large molecules.

Cartilage Flexible tissue, made of protein, that supports the skeleton.

Cells Tiny, living units that make up the human body. There are many different types of cell – such as nerve cells, blood cells, and muscle cells – each designed to carry out a specific task.

Cholesterol A waxy substance formed by the liver and present in foods such as egg yolks and animal fats. When cholesterol builds up in the arteries it can block them, leading to heart disease.

Fat A major type of nutrient that is stored in the body's tissues for use as energy. Fats contain more energy than carbohydrates but cannot be used as easily.

Fibre Parts of food, especially fruit and vegetables, that are difficult or impossible to digest but important for health. Insoluble fibre is found in cereal husks. Soluble fibre is found in the cell walls of plants.

Free radicals Molecules produced by the body's metabolism. Free radicals react with other molecules and can attack and damage cells. They have been linked to a number of diseases, including cancer and heart disease. Cigarette smoke, stress, illness, sunlight and other factors can cause over-production of free radicals.

Genes Characteristics are passed on from parents to children by genes – chemical instructions carried inside the body's cells.

Growth spurt The increase in height and weight – that comes before adolescence.

Immune system The cells and substances in the body that protect it against disease and ill-health.

Metabolism The normal chemical processes that occur in the body.

Mineral A type of minor nutrient needed by the body for many vital processes. Iron and calcium are both important minerals.

Nutrients Substances found in food that the body needs to stay healthy. The three main nutrients – fat, protein and carbohydrate – are known as macronutrients. Vitamins, minerals and other nutrients needed by the body in small quantities are known as micronutrients.

Oils Fats that are liquid at room temperature.

Phytochemicals Substances found in plants, vegetables, herbs and fruit that actively protect the body against disease.

Protein A type of major nutrient. Proteins consists of amino acids joined together. Their many jobs include growth and muscle formation and chemical reactions in the body's cells.

Starch A complex carbohydrate found in foods such as potatoes and cereals.

Sugar A simple carbohydrate found in fruit, sweets, and other foods. The body can break down sugar more quickly than starch.

Tissue Cells of the same kind are grouped together to form material called tissue. Bones, cartilages and muscles are all made of different types of tissue.

Vitamins Nutrients that the body needs in small quantities to control chemical reactions in cells. Vitamins also actively protect against certain diseases such as heart disease and cancer.

FURTHER INFORMATION

FURTHER READING

Health and Food by D. Baldwin, (Wayland, 1987)
We're Talking about Vegetarianism by Samantha Calvert (Wayland, 1997)
Eat Well by Miram Moss, (Wayland, 1992)
Diet and Health by Ida Weekes (Wayland, 1991)
What's the Big Idea: Food by Emily Moore (Hodder, 1999)
Exercise by Judy Sadgrove (Wayland, 1999)

USEFUL ADDRESSES

British Nutrition Foundation,
High Holborn House,
52–54 High Holborn,
London WC1V 6RQ
Tel: 020 7404 6504
Web page:
http:www.nutrition.org.uk
Publishes a range of information sheets and leaflets. 'Food – a fact of life' is a progressive food and nutrition programme for schools suitable for pupils aged 5–16 years. Key stage 3/4 packs *Energy and Nutrients*, *Diet and Health* and *Food Technology* are aimed at 11–16 years.

Food and Farming
    Education Service,
National Agriculture Centre,
Stoneleigh Park,
Warks CV8 2LZ
Tel: 01203 535707
Web page: http://cla.org.uk/ffes
A comprehensive site of teaching resources and information on food and farm visits and free material.

Health Education Authority,
Trevelyan House,
30 Great Peter Street,
London SW1P 2HW
Tel: 020 7222 5300
Web page: http://www.hea.org.uk

The Healthy Alliance,
Equinox South,
Great Park Road,
Almondsbury,
Bristol BS12 4BR
Tel: 01454 201686
A group that aims to help the South Asian community in the UK to achieve a healthy, balanced diet. Produces a range of leaflets, posters and other educational materials.

Kelloggs Company,
Kellogg Building,
Talbot Road,
Manchester M16 0PU
Tel 0161 869 2000
Web page:
http.www.kelloggs.co.uk
Nutritional information.

National Dairy Council,
Information Services Department,
5–7 John Princes Street,
London W1M 0AP
Tel: 020 7499 7822
Web page: http://www.milk.co.uk
The NDC publishes a range of useful leaflets including *Principles of a Balanced Diet*, and *Making Sense of Food*, *Make a Meal of it.*

Soil Association,
Bristol House,
Victoria Street,
Bristol BS1 6DF
Tel: 0117 929 0661
Web page:
http://www.soilassociation.org
Information on organic food and farming. Education pack available.

Vegetarian Society,
Parkdale,
Dunham Road,
Altrincham,
Cheshire WA14 4OG
Tel: 0161 928 0793
Web page: http://www.vegsoc.org
Wide range of information, fact sheets and project books.

INDEX